M000105230

THIS JOURNAL
BELONGS TO
AN AWESOME
BOY CALLED

M  T  W  TH  F  S  SU    DATE: __ / __ / __

## I AM THANKFUL FOR

1. _____
2. _____
3. _____

## SOMEONE SPECIAL TO ME & WHY

_____

I FEEL  ☐  ☐  ☐  ☐  ☐  ☐

## WHAT WAS GREAT ABOUT TODAY?

_____
_____
_____
_____
_____

DOODLE OF THE DAY!

M   T   W   TH   F   S   SU      DATE: ___/___/___

## I AM THANKFUL FOR

1. _____
2. _____
3. _____

## SOMEONE SPECIAL TO ME & WHY

_____

I FEEL   ☐   ☐   ☐   ☐   ☐   ☐

## WHAT WAS GREAT ABOUT TODAY?

_____
_____
_____
_____
_____

DOODLE OF THE DAY!

M  T  W  TH  F  S  SU      DATE: __/__/__

## I AM THANKFUL FOR

1. _____
2. _____
3. _____

## SOMEONE SPECIAL TO ME & WHY

_____

I FEEL  ☐  ☐  ☐  ☐  ☐  ☐

## WHAT WAS GREAT ABOUT TODAY?

_____
_____
_____
_____
_____

DOODLE OF THE DAY!

| M | T | W | TH | F | S | SU | DATE: ___/___/___ |

## I AM THANKFUL FOR

1. _____
2. _____
3. _____

## SOMEONE SPECIAL TO ME & WHY

_____

I FEEL ☐ ☐ ☐ ☐ ☐ ☐

## WHAT WAS GREAT ABOUT TODAY?

_____
_____
_____
_____
_____

DOODLE OF THE DAY!

# M T W TH F S SU    DATE: ___ / ___ / ___

## I AM THANKFUL FOR

1. _____
2. _____
3. _____

## SOMEONE SPECIAL TO ME & WHY

_____

## I FEEL

☐  ☐  ☐  ☐  ☐  ☐

## WHAT WAS GREAT ABOUT TODAY?

_____
_____
_____
_____
_____

DOODLE OF THE DAY!

M   T   W   TH   F   S   SU       DATE: ___ / ___ / ___

## I AM THANKFUL FOR

1. _____
2. _____
3. _____

## SOMEONE SPECIAL TO ME & WHY

_____

## I FEEL

☐   ☐   ☐   ☐   ☐   ☐

## WHAT WAS GREAT ABOUT TODAY?

_____
_____
_____
_____
_____

DOODLE OF THE DAY!

M T W TH F S SU     DATE: __ / __ / __

## I AM THANKFUL FOR

1. _____
2. _____
3. _____

## SOMEONE SPECIAL TO ME & WHY

_____

## I FEEL

☐  ☐  ☐  ☐  ☐  ☐

## WHAT WAS GREAT ABOUT TODAY?

_____
_____
_____
_____
_____

DOODLE OF THE DAY!

M  T  W  TH  F  S  SU    DATE: __ / __ / __

## I AM THANKFUL FOR

1. _____
2. _____
3. _____

## SOMEONE SPECIAL TO ME & WHY

_____

## I FEEL

☐  ☐  ☐  ☐  ☐  ☐

## WHAT WAS GREAT ABOUT TODAY?

_____
_____
_____
_____
_____

DOODLE OF THE DAY!

M  T  W  TH  F  S  SU      DATE: ___ / ___ / ___

## I AM THANKFUL FOR

1. _____
2. _____
3. _____

## SOMEONE SPECIAL TO ME & WHY

_____

## I FEEL

☐  ☐  ☐  ☐  ☐  ☐

## WHAT WAS GREAT ABOUT TODAY?

_____
_____
_____
_____
_____

DOODLE OF THE DAY!

M  T  W  TH  F  S  SU      DATE: ___/___/___

## I AM THANKFUL FOR

1. _____
2. _____
3. _____

## SOMEONE SPECIAL TO ME & WHY

_____

I FEEL  ☐  ☐  ☐  ☐  ☐  ☐

## WHAT WAS GREAT ABOUT TODAY?

_____
_____
_____
_____
_____

DOODLE OF THE DAY!

M  T  W  TH  F  S  SU     DATE: ___/___/___

## I AM THANKFUL FOR

1. _____
2. _____
3. _____

## SOMEONE SPECIAL TO ME & WHY

_____

I FEEL  ☐  ☐  ☐  ☐  ☐  ☐

## WHAT WAS GREAT ABOUT TODAY?

_____
_____
_____
_____
_____

DOODLE OF THE DAY!

M  T  W  TH  F  S  SU    DATE: ___ / ___ / ___

## I AM THANKFUL FOR

1. _____
2. _____
3. _____

## SOMEONE SPECIAL TO ME & WHY

_____

## I FEEL

☐  ☐  ☐  ☐  ☐  ☐

## WHAT WAS GREAT ABOUT TODAY?

_____
_____
_____
_____

DOODLE OF THE DAY!

M   T   W   TH   F   S   SU      DATE: ___ / ___ / ___

## I AM THANKFUL FOR

1. _____
2. _____
3. _____

## SOMEONE SPECIAL TO ME & WHY

_____

I FEEL  ☐  ☐  ☐  ☐  ☐  ☐

## WHAT WAS GREAT ABOUT TODAY?

_____
_____
_____
_____
_____

DOODLE OF THE DAY!

M  T  W  TH  F  S  SU     DATE: ___ / ___ / ___

## I AM THANKFUL FOR

1. _____
2. _____
3. _____

## SOMEONE SPECIAL TO ME & WHY

_____

I FEEL  ☐  ☐  ☐  ☐  ☐  ☐

## WHAT WAS GREAT ABOUT TODAY?

_____
_____
_____
_____
_____

DOODLE OF THE DAY!

M  T  W  TH  F  S  SU     DATE: ___ / ___ / ___

## I AM THANKFUL FOR

1. _____
2. _____
3. _____

## SOMEONE SPECIAL TO ME & WHY

_____

**I FEEL** ☐  ☐  ☐  ☐  ☐  ☐

## WHAT WAS GREAT ABOUT TODAY?

_____
_____
_____
_____
_____

DOODLE OF THE DAY!

M  T  W  TH  F  S  SU       DATE: ___ / ___ / ___

## I AM THANKFUL FOR

1. _____

2. _____

3. _____

## SOMEONE SPECIAL TO ME & WHY

_____

I FEEL

## WHAT WAS GREAT ABOUT TODAY?

_____

_____

_____

_____

_____

DOODLE OF THE DAY!

## M  T  W  TH  F  S  SU        DATE: __/__/__

## I AM THANKFUL FOR

1. _____
2. _____
3. _____

## SOMEONE SPECIAL TO ME & WHY

_____

## I FEEL

☐  ☐  ☐  ☐  ☐  ☐

## WHAT WAS GREAT ABOUT TODAY?

_____
_____
_____
_____
_____

DOODLE OF THE DAY!

M  T  W  TH  F  S  SU      DATE: ___ / ___ / ___

## I AM THANKFUL FOR

1. _____
2. _____
3. _____

## SOMEONE SPECIAL TO ME & WHY

_____

## I FEEL

☐  ☐  ☐  ☐  ☐  ☐

## WHAT WAS GREAT ABOUT TODAY?

_____
_____
_____
_____

DOODLE OF THE DAY!

M   T   W   TH   F   S   SU      DATE: __/__/__

## I AM THANKFUL FOR

1. _____
2. _____
3. _____

## SOMEONE SPECIAL TO ME & WHY

_____

I FEEL  ☐  ☐  ☐  ☐  ☐  ☐

## WHAT WAS GREAT ABOUT TODAY?

_____
_____
_____
_____
_____

DOODLE OF THE DAY!

M  T  W  TH  F  S  SU     DATE: ___ / ___ / ___

## I AM THANKFUL FOR

1. _____
_____
2. _____
3. _____

## SOMEONE SPECIAL TO ME & WHY

_____

I FEEL  ☐  ☐  ☐  ☐  ☐  ☐

## WHAT WAS GREAT ABOUT TODAY?

_____
_____
_____
_____
_____

DOODLE OF THE DAY!

M  T  W  TH  F  S  SU     DATE: ___ / ___ / ___

## I AM THANKFUL FOR

1. _____
2. _____
3. _____

## SOMEONE SPECIAL TO ME & WHY

_____

## I FEEL

☐  ☐  ☐  ☐  ☐  ☐

## WHAT WAS GREAT ABOUT TODAY?

_____
_____
_____
_____
_____

DOODLE OF THE DAY!

M   T   W   TH   F   S   SU       DATE: ___/___/___

I AM THANKFUL FOR

1. _____
2. _____
3. _____

SOMEONE SPECIAL TO ME & WHY

_____

I FEEL   ☐   ☐   ☐   ☐   ☐   ☐

WHAT WAS GREAT ABOUT TODAY?

_____
_____
_____
_____
_____

DOODLE OF THE DAY!

M  T  W  TH  F  S  SU     DATE: ___ / ___ / ___

## I AM THANKFUL FOR

1. _____
2. _____
3. _____

## SOMEONE SPECIAL TO ME & WHY

_____

I FEEL  ☐  ☐  ☐  ☐  ☐  ☐

## WHAT WAS GREAT ABOUT TODAY?

_____
_____
_____
_____
_____

DOODLE OF THE DAY!

## M  T  W  TH  F  S  SU     DATE: __/__/__

## I AM THANKFUL FOR

1. _____
2. _____
3. _____

## SOMEONE SPECIAL TO ME & WHY

_____

## I FEEL

☐  ☐  ☐  ☐  ☐  ☐

## WHAT WAS GREAT ABOUT TODAY?

_____
_____
_____
_____
_____

DOODLE OF THE DAY!

M  T  W  TH  F  S  SU       DATE: ___/___/___

## I AM THANKFUL FOR

1. _____
   _____
2. _____
   _____
3. _____
   _____

## SOMEONE SPECIAL TO ME & WHY

_____

## I FEEL  ☐  ☐  ☐  ☐  ☐  ☐

## WHAT WAS GREAT ABOUT TODAY?

_____
_____
_____
_____
_____

DOODLE OF THE DAY!

# M  T  W  TH  F  S  SU    DATE: ___/___/___

## I AM THANKFUL FOR

1. _____
2. _____
3. _____

## SOMEONE SPECIAL TO ME & WHY

_____

## I FEEL

☐  ☐  ☐  ☐  ☐  ☐

## WHAT WAS GREAT ABOUT TODAY?

_____
_____
_____
_____
_____

DOODLE OF THE DAY!

M  T  W  TH  F  S  SU     DATE: ___/___/___

## I AM THANKFUL FOR

1. _____
2. _____
3. _____

## SOMEONE SPECIAL TO ME & WHY

_____

## I FEEL

☐  ☐  ☐  ☐  ☐  ☐

## WHAT WAS GREAT ABOUT TODAY?

_____
_____
_____
_____
_____

DOODLE OF THE DAY!

M  T  W  TH  F  S  SU     DATE: ___ / ___ / ___

## I AM THANKFUL FOR

1. _____
2. _____
3. _____

## SOMEONE SPECIAL TO ME & WHY

_____

I FEEL  ☐  ☐  ☐  ☐  ☐  ☐

## WHAT WAS GREAT ABOUT TODAY?

_____
_____
_____
_____

DOODLE OF THE DAY!

M  T  W  TH  F  S  SU     DATE: ___ / ___ / ___

## I AM THANKFUL FOR

1. _____
2. _____
3. _____

## SOMEONE SPECIAL TO ME & WHY

_____

## I FEEL
☐  ☐  ☐  ☐  ☐  ☐

## WHAT WAS GREAT ABOUT TODAY?

_____
_____
_____
_____
_____

DOODLE OF THE DAY!

M  T  W  TH  F  S  SU     DATE: ___/___/___

## I AM THANKFUL FOR

1. _____
_____
2. _____
3. _____

## SOMEONE SPECIAL TO ME & WHY

_____

I FEEL  ☐  ☐  ☐  ☐  ☐  ☐

## WHAT WAS GREAT ABOUT TODAY?

_____
_____
_____
_____
_____

DOODLE OF THE DAY!

M  T  W  TH  F  S  SU     DATE: ___ / ___ / ___

## I AM THANKFUL FOR

1. _____
2. _____
3. _____

## SOMEONE SPECIAL TO ME & WHY

_____

## I FEEL

☐  ☐  ☐  ☐  ☐  ☐

## WHAT WAS GREAT ABOUT TODAY?

_____
_____
_____
_____
_____

DOODLE OF THE DAY!

M  T  W  TH  F  S  SU    DATE: ___ / ___ / ___

## I AM THANKFUL FOR

1. _____
2. _____
3. _____

## SOMEONE SPECIAL TO ME & WHY

_____

## I FEEL

☐  ☐  ☐  ☐  ☐  ☐

## WHAT WAS GREAT ABOUT TODAY?

_____
_____
_____
_____
_____

DOODLE OF THE DAY!

# M T W TH F S SU    DATE: __/__/__

## I AM THANKFUL FOR

1. _____
2. _____
3. _____

## SOMEONE SPECIAL TO ME & WHY

_____

## I FEEL

☐ ☐ ☐ ☐ ☐ ☐

## WHAT WAS GREAT ABOUT TODAY?

_____
_____
_____
_____
_____

DOODLE OF THE DAY!

M   T   W   TH   F   S   SU     DATE: ___ / ___ / ___

## I AM THANKFUL FOR

1. _____
2. _____
3. _____

## SOMEONE SPECIAL TO ME & WHY

_____

## I FEEL

☐   ☐   ☐   ☐   ☐   ☐

## WHAT WAS GREAT ABOUT TODAY?

_____
_____
_____
_____
_____

DOODLE OF THE DAY!

| M | T | W | TH | F | S | SU | DATE: __/__/__ |

## I AM THANKFUL FOR

1. _____
2. _____
3. _____

## SOMEONE SPECIAL TO ME & WHY

_____

## I FEEL

☐ ☐ ☐ ☐ ☐ ☐

## WHAT WAS GREAT ABOUT TODAY?

_____
_____
_____
_____
_____

DOODLE OF THE DAY!

M T W TH F S SU       DATE: __ / __ / __

## I AM THANKFUL FOR

1. _____
2. _____
3. _____

## SOMEONE SPECIAL TO ME & WHY

_____

I FEEL  ☐  ☐  ☐  ☐  ☐  ☐

## WHAT WAS GREAT ABOUT TODAY?

_____
_____
_____
_____
_____

DOODLE OF THE DAY!

M  T  W  TH  F  S  SU     DATE: ___/___/___

## I AM THANKFUL FOR

1. _____
2. _____
3. _____

## SOMEONE SPECIAL TO ME & WHY

_____

## I FEEL

☐  ☐  ☐  ☐  ☐  ☐

## WHAT WAS GREAT ABOUT TODAY?

_____
_____
_____
_____
_____

DOODLE OF THE DAY!

M   T   W   TH   F   S   SU       DATE: ___ / ___ / ___

## I AM THANKFUL FOR

1. _____
_____
2. _____
_____
3. _____

## SOMEONE SPECIAL TO ME & WHY

_____

I FEEL   ☐   ☐   ☐   ☐   ☐   ☐

## WHAT WAS GREAT ABOUT TODAY?

_____
_____
_____
_____
_____

DOODLE OF THE DAY!

M   T   W   TH   F   S   SU       DATE: ___ / ___ / ___

## I AM THANKFUL FOR

1. _____

2. _____

3. _____

## SOMEONE SPECIAL TO ME & WHY

_____

I FEEL   ☐   ☐   ☐   ☐   ☐   ☐

## WHAT WAS GREAT ABOUT TODAY?

_____

_____

_____

_____

_____

DOODLE OF THE DAY!

M  T  W  TH  F  S  SU     DATE: ___/___/___

## I AM THANKFUL FOR

1. _____
2. _____
3. _____

## SOMEONE SPECIAL TO ME & WHY

_____

I FEEL  ☐  ☐  ☐  ☐  ☐  ☐

## WHAT WAS GREAT ABOUT TODAY?

_____
_____
_____
_____
_____

DOODLE OF THE DAY!

M  T  W  TH  F  S  SU    DATE: ___ / ___ / ___

## I AM THANKFUL FOR

1. _____
2. _____
3. _____

## SOMEONE SPECIAL TO ME & WHY

_____

I FEEL  ☐  ☐  ☐  ☐  ☐  ☐

## WHAT WAS GREAT ABOUT TODAY?

_____
_____
_____
_____
_____

DOODLE OF THE DAY!

M  T  W  TH  F  S  SU     DATE: __ / __ / __

## I AM THANKFUL FOR

1. _____
2. _____
3. _____

## SOMEONE SPECIAL TO ME & WHY

_____

I FEEL  ☐  ☐  ☐  ☐  ☐  ☐

## WHAT WAS GREAT ABOUT TODAY?

_____
_____
_____
_____
_____

DOODLE OF THE DAY!

M T W TH F S SU    DATE: ___ / ___ / ___

## I AM THANKFUL FOR

1. _____
2. _____
3. _____

## SOMEONE SPECIAL TO ME & WHY

_____

## I FEEL

☐ ☐ ☐ ☐ ☐ ☐

## WHAT WAS GREAT ABOUT TODAY?

_____
_____
_____
_____
_____

DOODLE OF THE DAY!

M  T  W  TH  F  S  SU     DATE: ___ / ___ / ___

## I AM THANKFUL FOR

1. _____
2. _____
3. _____

## SOMEONE SPECIAL TO ME & WHY

_____

I FEEL  ☐  ☐  ☐  ☐  ☐  ☐

## WHAT WAS GREAT ABOUT TODAY?

_____
_____
_____
_____
_____

DOODLE OF THE DAY!

M  T  W  TH  F  S  SU     DATE: ___ / ___ / ___

## I AM THANKFUL FOR

1. _____
2. _____
3. _____

## SOMEONE SPECIAL TO ME & WHY

_____

## I FEEL

☐  ☐  ☐  ☐  ☐  ☐

## WHAT WAS GREAT ABOUT TODAY?

_____
_____
_____
_____
_____

DOODLE OF THE DAY!

M  T  W  TH  F  S  SU     DATE: ___ / ___ / ___

## I AM THANKFUL FOR

1. _____
2. _____
3. _____

## SOMEONE SPECIAL TO ME & WHY

_____

## I FEEL

☐  ☐  ☐  ☐  ☐  ☐

## WHAT WAS GREAT ABOUT TODAY?

_____
_____
_____
_____
_____

DOODLE OF THE DAY!

M  T  W  TH  F  S  SU      DATE: ___ / ___ / ___

## I AM THANKFUL FOR

1. _____
2. _____
3. _____

## SOMEONE SPECIAL TO ME & WHY

_____

## I FEEL

☐  ☐  ☐  ☐  ☐  ☐

## WHAT WAS GREAT ABOUT TODAY?

_____
_____
_____
_____
_____

DOODLE OF THE DAY!

M  T  W  TH  F  S  SU    DATE: __ / __ / __

## I AM THANKFUL FOR

1. _____
2. _____
3. _____

## SOMEONE SPECIAL TO ME & WHY

_____

## I FEEL

☐  ☐  ☐  ☐  ☐  ☐

## WHAT WAS GREAT ABOUT TODAY?

_____
_____
_____
_____

DOODLE OF THE DAY!

M  T  W  TH  F  S  SU        DATE: ___ / ___ / ___

## I AM THANKFUL FOR

1. _____
2. _____
3. _____

## SOMEONE SPECIAL TO ME & WHY

_____

I FEEL  ☐  ☐  ☐  ☐  ☐  ☐

## WHAT WAS GREAT ABOUT TODAY?

_____
_____
_____
_____
_____

DOODLE OF THE DAY!

M  T  W  TH  F  S  SU    DATE: ___/___/___

## I AM THANKFUL FOR

1. _____
2. _____
3. _____

## SOMEONE SPECIAL TO ME & WHY

_____

## I FEEL

☐  ☐  ☐  ☐  ☐  ☐

## WHAT WAS GREAT ABOUT TODAY?

_____
_____
_____
_____
_____

DOODLE OF THE DAY!

M  T  W  TH  F  S  SU    DATE: ___/___/___

## I AM THANKFUL FOR

1. _____
2. _____
3. _____

## SOMEONE SPECIAL TO ME & WHY

_____

## I FEEL
☐  ☐  ☐  ☐  ☐  ☐

## WHAT WAS GREAT ABOUT TODAY?

_____
_____
_____
_____
_____

DOODLE OF THE DAY!

## M  T  W  TH  F  S  SU          DATE: __/__/__

### I AM THANKFUL FOR

1. _____
2. _____
3. _____

### SOMEONE SPECIAL TO ME & WHY

_____

### I FEEL ☐ ☐ ☐ ☐ ☐ ☐

### WHAT WAS GREAT ABOUT TODAY?

_____
_____
_____
_____
_____

DOODLE OF THE DAY!

M  T  W  TH  F  S  SU     DATE: __/__/__

## I AM THANKFUL FOR

1. _____
2. _____
3. _____

## SOMEONE SPECIAL TO ME & WHY

_____

## I FEEL

☐  ☐  ☐  ☐  ☐  ☐

## WHAT WAS GREAT ABOUT TODAY?

_____
_____
_____
_____
_____

DOODLE OF THE DAY!

M   T   W   TH   F   S   SU      DATE: ___ / ___ / ___

## I AM THANKFUL FOR

1. _____
2. _____
3. _____

## SOMEONE SPECIAL TO ME & WHY

_____

I FEEL   ☐   ☐   ☐   ☐   ☐   ☐

## WHAT WAS GREAT ABOUT TODAY?

_____

_____

_____

_____

_____

DOODLE OF THE DAY!

M   T   W   TH   F   S   SU        DATE: ___ / ___ / ___

## I AM THANKFUL FOR

1. _____
2. _____
3. _____

## SOMEONE SPECIAL TO ME & WHY

_____

## I FEEL

☐   ☐   ☐   ☐   ☐   ☐

## WHAT WAS GREAT ABOUT TODAY?

_____
_____
_____
_____
_____

DOODLE OF THE DAY!

M  T  W  TH  F  S  SU        DATE: __ / __ / __

## I AM THANKFUL FOR

1. _____
2. _____
3. _____

## SOMEONE SPECIAL TO ME & WHY

_____

I FEEL  ☐  ☐  ☐  ☐  ☐  ☐

## WHAT WAS GREAT ABOUT TODAY?

_____
_____
_____
_____

DOODLE OF THE DAY!

M  T  W  TH  F  S  SU     DATE: ___ / ___ / ___

## I AM THANKFUL FOR

1. _____
2. _____
3. _____

## SOMEONE SPECIAL TO ME & WHY

_____

I FEEL   ☐  ☐  ☐  ☐  ☐  ☐

## WHAT WAS GREAT ABOUT TODAY?

_____
_____
_____
_____
_____

DOODLE OF THE DAY!

M  T  W  TH  F  S  SU       DATE: ___/___/___

## I AM THANKFUL FOR

1. _____
2. _____
3. _____

## SOMEONE SPECIAL TO ME & WHY

_____

I FEEL ☐ ☐ ☐ ☐ ☐ ☐

## WHAT WAS GREAT ABOUT TODAY?

_____
_____
_____
_____
_____

DOODLE OF THE DAY!

M  T  W  TH  F  S  SU     DATE: ___/___/___

## I AM THANKFUL FOR

1. _____
2. _____
3. _____

## SOMEONE SPECIAL TO ME & WHY

_____

I FEEL  ☐  ☐  ☐  ☐  ☐  ☐

## WHAT WAS GREAT ABOUT TODAY?

_____
_____
_____
_____
_____

DOODLE OF THE DAY!

M   T   W   TH   F   S   SU          DATE: ___ / ___ / ___

## I AM THANKFUL FOR

1. _____

2. _____

3. _____

## SOMEONE SPECIAL TO ME & WHY

_____

I FEEL   ☐   ☐   ☐   ☐   ☐   ☐

## WHAT WAS GREAT ABOUT TODAY?

_____

_____

_____

_____

_____

DOODLE OF THE DAY!

M  T  W  TH  F  S  SU     DATE: ___ / ___ / ___

## I AM THANKFUL FOR

1. _____
2. _____
3. _____

## SOMEONE SPECIAL TO ME & WHY

_____

## I FEEL

☐  ☐  ☐  ☐  ☐  ☐

## WHAT WAS GREAT ABOUT TODAY?

_____
_____
_____
_____
_____

DOODLE OF THE DAY!

# M  T  W  TH  F  S  SU     DATE: ___ / ___ / ___

## I AM THANKFUL FOR

1. _____

2. _____

3. _____

## SOMEONE SPECIAL TO ME & WHY

_____

## I FEEL

☐   ☐   ☐   ☐   ☐   ☐

## WHAT WAS GREAT ABOUT TODAY?

_____

_____

_____

_____

_____

DOODLE OF THE DAY!

M  T  W  TH  F  S  SU     DATE: __ / __ / __

## I AM THANKFUL FOR

1. _____
2. _____
3. _____

## SOMEONE SPECIAL TO ME & WHY

_____

## I FEEL

☐  ☐  ☐  ☐  ☐  ☐

## WHAT WAS GREAT ABOUT TODAY?

_____
_____
_____
_____
_____

DOODLE OF THE DAY!

M  T  W  TH  F  S  SU        DATE: ___ / ___ / ___

## I AM THANKFUL FOR

1. _____
2. _____
3. _____

## SOMEONE SPECIAL TO ME & WHY

_____

I FEEL  □  □  □  □  □  □

## WHAT WAS GREAT ABOUT TODAY?

_____
_____
_____
_____

DOODLE OF THE DAY!

M   T   W   TH   F   S   SU      DATE: __/__/__

## I AM THANKFUL FOR

1. _____
2. _____
3. _____

## SOMEONE SPECIAL TO ME & WHY

_____

**I FEEL**  ☐  ☐  ☐  ☐  ☐  ☐

## WHAT WAS GREAT ABOUT TODAY?

_____
_____
_____
_____
_____

DOODLE OF THE DAY!

M  T  W  TH  F  S  SU     DATE: ___ / ___ / ___

## I AM THANKFUL FOR

1. _____
2. _____
3. _____

## SOMEONE SPECIAL TO ME & WHY

_____

I FEEL  ☐  ☐  ☐  ☐  ☐  ☐

## WHAT WAS GREAT ABOUT TODAY?

_____
_____
_____
_____
_____

DOODLE OF THE DAY!

M  T  W  TH  F  S  SU     DATE: __ / __ / __

## I AM THANKFUL FOR

1. _____
2. _____
3. _____

## SOMEONE SPECIAL TO ME & WHY

_____

## I FEEL

☐  ☐  ☐  ☐  ☐  ☐

## WHAT WAS GREAT ABOUT TODAY?

_____
_____
_____
_____
_____

DOODLE OF THE DAY!

M  T  W  TH  F  S  SU     DATE: ___/___/___

## I AM THANKFUL FOR

1. _____
2. _____
3. _____

## SOMEONE SPECIAL TO ME & WHY

_____

## I FEEL

☐  ☐  ☐  ☐  ☐  ☐

## WHAT WAS GREAT ABOUT TODAY?

_____
_____
_____
_____
_____

DOODLE OF THE DAY!

M  T  W  TH  F  S  SU    DATE: ___ / ___ / ___

## I AM THANKFUL FOR

1. _____
2. _____
3. _____

## SOMEONE SPECIAL TO ME & WHY

_____

## I FEEL

☐  ☐  ☐  ☐  ☐  ☐

## WHAT WAS GREAT ABOUT TODAY?

_____
_____
_____
_____
_____

DOODLE OF THE DAY!

M  T  W  TH  F  S  SU     DATE: ___/___/___

## I AM THANKFUL FOR

1. _____
2. _____
3. _____

## SOMEONE SPECIAL TO ME & WHY

_____

## I FEEL

☐  ☐  ☐  ☐  ☐  ☐

## WHAT WAS GREAT ABOUT TODAY?

_____
_____
_____
_____
_____

DOODLE OF THE DAY!

M T W TH F S SU DATE: __ / __ / __

## I AM THANKFUL FOR

1. _____
2. _____
3. _____

## SOMEONE SPECIAL TO ME & WHY

_____

## I FEEL

☐ ☐ ☐ ☐ ☐ ☐

## WHAT WAS GREAT ABOUT TODAY?

_____
_____
_____
_____
_____

DOODLE OF THE DAY!

M  T  W  TH  F  S  SU     DATE: __ / __ / __

## I AM THANKFUL FOR

1. _____
2. _____
3. _____

## SOMEONE SPECIAL TO ME & WHY

_____

I FEEL  ☐  ☐  ☐  ☐  ☐  ☐

## WHAT WAS GREAT ABOUT TODAY?

_____
_____
_____
_____
_____

DOODLE OF THE DAY!

M  T  W  TH  F  S  SU      DATE: __ / __ / __

## I AM THANKFUL FOR

1. _____
2. _____
3. _____

## SOMEONE SPECIAL TO ME & WHY

_____

I FEEL  ☐  ☐  ☐  ☐  ☐  ☐

## WHAT WAS GREAT ABOUT TODAY?

_____
_____
_____
_____
_____

DOODLE OF THE DAY!

# M T W TH F S SU    DATE: __ / __ / __

## I AM THANKFUL FOR

1. _____
2. _____
3. _____

## SOMEONE SPECIAL TO ME & WHY

_____

## I FEEL

☐ ☐ ☐ ☐ ☐ ☐

## WHAT WAS GREAT ABOUT TODAY?

_____
_____
_____
_____

DOODLE OF THE DAY!

M T W TH F S SU     DATE: ___/___/___

## I AM THANKFUL FOR

1. _____
2. _____
3. _____

## SOMEONE SPECIAL TO ME & WHY

_____

## I FEEL

☐ ☐ ☐ ☐ ☐ ☐

## WHAT WAS GREAT ABOUT TODAY?

_____
_____
_____
_____
_____

DOODLE OF THE DAY!

M T W TH F S SU     DATE: __/__/__

## I AM THANKFUL FOR

1. _____
2. _____
3. _____

## SOMEONE SPECIAL TO ME & WHY

_____

## I FEEL

☐  ☐  ☐  ☐  ☐  ☐

## WHAT WAS GREAT ABOUT TODAY?

_____
_____
_____
_____
_____

DOODLE OF THE DAY!

M  T  W  TH  F  S  SU     DATE: __/__/__

## I AM THANKFUL FOR

1. _____
2. _____
3. _____

## SOMEONE SPECIAL TO ME & WHY

_____

## I FEEL

☐  ☐  ☐  ☐  ☐  ☐

## WHAT WAS GREAT ABOUT TODAY?

_____
_____
_____
_____
_____

DOODLE OF THE DAY!

M  T  W  TH  F  S  SU     DATE: ___ / ___ / ___

## I AM THANKFUL FOR

1. _____
2. _____
3. _____

## SOMEONE SPECIAL TO ME & WHY

_____

## I FEEL

☐  ☐  ☐  ☐  ☐  ☐

## WHAT WAS GREAT ABOUT TODAY?

_____
_____
_____
_____
_____

DOODLE OF THE DAY!

**M  T  W  TH  F  S  SU     DATE: __/__/__**

## I AM THANKFUL FOR

1. _____
2. _____
3. _____

## SOMEONE SPECIAL TO ME & WHY
_____

**I FEEL**  ☐  ☐  ☐  ☐  ☐  ☐

## WHAT WAS GREAT ABOUT TODAY?

_____
_____
_____
_____
_____

DOODLE OF THE DAY!

M  T  W  TH  F  S  SU      DATE: __ / __ / __

## I AM THANKFUL FOR

1. _____
_____
2. _____
_____
3. _____
_____

## SOMEONE SPECIAL TO ME & WHY

_____

I FEEL  ☐  ☐  ☐  ☐  ☐  ☐

## WHAT WAS GREAT ABOUT TODAY?

_____
_____
_____
_____
_____

DOODLE OF THE DAY!

# M T W TH F S SU     DATE: __/__/__

## I AM THANKFUL FOR

1. _____
2. _____
3. _____

## SOMEONE SPECIAL TO ME & WHY

_____

## I FEEL

☐ ☐ ☐ ☐ ☐ ☐

## WHAT WAS GREAT ABOUT TODAY?

_____
_____
_____
_____
_____

**DOODLE OF THE DAY!**

## M  T  W  TH  F  S  SU     DATE: ___ / ___ / ___

## I AM THANKFUL FOR

1. _____
2. _____
3. _____

## SOMEONE SPECIAL TO ME & WHY

_____

## I FEEL

☐ ☐ ☐ ☐ ☐ ☐

## WHAT WAS GREAT ABOUT TODAY?

_____

_____

_____

_____

_____

DOODLE OF THE DAY!

M  T  W  TH  F  S  SU     DATE: ___ / ___ / ___

## I AM THANKFUL FOR

1. _____
2. _____
3. _____

## SOMEONE SPECIAL TO ME & WHY

_____

## I FEEL

☐  ☐  ☐  ☐  ☐  ☐

## WHAT WAS GREAT ABOUT TODAY?

_____
_____
_____
_____
_____

DOODLE OF THE DAY!

M  T  W  TH  F  S  SU     DATE: __ / __ / __

## I AM THANKFUL FOR

1. _____
2. _____
3. _____

## SOMEONE SPECIAL TO ME & WHY

_____

I FEEL  ☐  ☐  ☐  ☐  ☐  ☐

## WHAT WAS GREAT ABOUT TODAY?

_____
_____
_____
_____
_____

DOODLE OF THE DAY!

M   T   W   TH   F   S   SU        DATE: ___ / ___ / ___

## I AM THANKFUL FOR

1. _____
2. _____
3. _____

## SOMEONE SPECIAL TO ME & WHY

_____

## I FEEL

☐   ☐   ☐   ☐   ☐   ☐

## WHAT WAS GREAT ABOUT TODAY?

_____
_____
_____
_____
_____

DOODLE OF THE DAY!

M  T  W  TH  F  S  SU        DATE: __ / __ / __

## I AM THANKFUL FOR

1. _____
2. _____
3. _____

## SOMEONE SPECIAL TO ME & WHY

_____

I FEEL  ☐  ☐  ☐  ☐  ☐  ☐

## WHAT WAS GREAT ABOUT TODAY?

_____
_____
_____
_____
_____

DOODLE OF THE DAY!

M  T  W  TH  F  S  SU      DATE: ___ / ___ / ___

## I AM THANKFUL FOR

1. _____
2. _____
3. _____

## SOMEONE SPECIAL TO ME & WHY

_____

I FEEL  ☐  ☐  ☐  ☐  ☐  ☐

## WHAT WAS GREAT ABOUT TODAY?

_____
_____
_____
_____
_____

DOODLE OF THE DAY!

M  T  W  TH  F  S  SU     DATE: __ / __ / __

## I AM THANKFUL FOR

1. _____
_____
2. _____
_____
3. _____
_____

## SOMEONE SPECIAL TO ME & WHY

_____

I FEEL  ☐  ☐  ☐  ☐  ☐  ☐

## WHAT WAS GREAT ABOUT TODAY?

_____
_____
_____
_____
_____

DOODLE OF THE DAY!

M  T  W  TH  F  S  SU     DATE: __/__/__

## I AM THANKFUL FOR

1. _____
2. _____
3. _____

## SOMEONE SPECIAL TO ME & WHY

_____

I FEEL  ☐  ☐  ☐  ☐  ☐  ☐

## WHAT WAS GREAT ABOUT TODAY?

_____
_____
_____
_____
_____

DOODLE OF THE DAY!

M  T  W  TH  F  S  SU     DATE: ___/___/___

## I AM THANKFUL FOR

1. _____
2. _____
3. _____

## SOMEONE SPECIAL TO ME & WHY

_____

I FEEL  ☐  ☐  ☐  ☐  ☐  ☐

## WHAT WAS GREAT ABOUT TODAY?

_____
_____
_____
_____
_____

DOODLE OF THE DAY!

M  T  W  TH  F  S  SU    DATE: ___ / ___ / ___

## I AM THANKFUL FOR

1. _____
2. _____
3. _____

## SOMEONE SPECIAL TO ME & WHY

_____

I FEEL  ☐  ☐  ☐  ☐  ☐  ☐

## WHAT WAS GREAT ABOUT TODAY?

_____
_____
_____
_____
_____

DOODLE OF THE DAY!

M  T  W  TH  F  S  SU    DATE: ___ / ___ / ___

## I AM THANKFUL FOR

1. _____
2. _____
3. _____

## SOMEONE SPECIAL TO ME & WHY

_____

## I FEEL

☐  ☐  ☐  ☐  ☐  ☐

## WHAT WAS GREAT ABOUT TODAY?

_____
_____
_____
_____
_____

DOODLE OF THE DAY!

M   T   W   TH   F   S   SU        DATE: ___ / ___ / ___

## I AM THANKFUL FOR

1. _____
2. _____
3. _____

## SOMEONE SPECIAL TO ME & WHY

_____

I FEEL  ☐  ☐  ☐  ☐  ☐  ☐

## WHAT WAS GREAT ABOUT TODAY?

_____
_____
_____
_____
_____

DOODLE OF THE DAY!

M  T  W  TH  F  S  SU     DATE: ___ / ___ / ___

## I AM THANKFUL FOR

1. _____
2. _____
3. _____

## SOMEONE SPECIAL TO ME & WHY

_____

I FEEL  ☐  ☐  ☐  ☐  ☐  ☐

## WHAT WAS GREAT ABOUT TODAY?

_____
_____
_____
_____
_____

DOODLE OF THE DAY!

M  T  W  TH  F  S  SU      DATE: ___/___/___

## I AM THANKFUL FOR

1. _____
2. _____
3. _____

## SOMEONE SPECIAL TO ME & WHY

_____

I FEEL  ☐  ☐  ☐  ☐  ☐  ☐

## WHAT WAS GREAT ABOUT TODAY?

_____
_____
_____
_____
_____

DOODLE OF THE DAY!

| M T W TH F S SU | DATE: ___ / ___ / ___ |

## I AM THANKFUL FOR

1. _____
2. _____
3. _____

## SOMEONE SPECIAL TO ME & WHY

_____

**I FEEL** ☐ ☐ ☐ ☐ ☐ ☐

## WHAT WAS GREAT ABOUT TODAY?

_____
_____
_____
_____
_____

**DOODLE OF THE DAY!**

M  T  W  TH  F  S  SU     DATE: ___ / ___ / ___

## I AM THANKFUL FOR

1. _____
2. _____
3. _____

## SOMEONE SPECIAL TO ME & WHY

_____

## I FEEL

☐  ☐  ☐  ☐  ☐  ☐

## WHAT WAS GREAT ABOUT TODAY?

_____
_____
_____
_____
_____

DOODLE OF THE DAY!

M  T  W  TH  F  S  SU     DATE: __ / __ / __

## I AM THANKFUL FOR

1. _____
2. _____
3. _____

## SOMEONE SPECIAL TO ME & WHY

_____

## I FEEL

□  □  □  □  □  □

## WHAT WAS GREAT ABOUT TODAY?

_____
_____
_____
_____
_____

DOODLE OF THE DAY!

M   T   W   TH   F   S   SU       DATE: ___ / ___ / ___

## I AM THANKFUL FOR

1. _____
2. _____
3. _____

## SOMEONE SPECIAL TO ME & WHY

_____

## I FEEL

☐   ☐   ☐   ☐   ☐   ☐

## WHAT WAS GREAT ABOUT TODAY?

_____
_____
_____
_____
_____

DOODLE OF THE DAY!

M  T  W  TH  F  S  SU     DATE: __ / __ / __

## I AM THANKFUL FOR

1. _____
2. _____
3. _____

## SOMEONE SPECIAL TO ME & WHY

_____

I FEEL   ☐   ☐   ☐   ☐   ☐   ☐

## WHAT WAS GREAT ABOUT TODAY?

_____
_____
_____
_____
_____

DOODLE OF THE DAY!

M  T  W  TH  F  S  SU      DATE: ___/___/___

## I AM THANKFUL FOR

1. _____
2. _____
3. _____

## SOMEONE SPECIAL TO ME & WHY

_____

I FEEL  ☐  ☐  ☐  ☐  ☐  ☐

## WHAT WAS GREAT ABOUT TODAY?

_____
_____
_____
_____
_____

DOODLE OF THE DAY!

M T W TH F S SU     DATE: ___ / ___ / ___

## I AM THANKFUL FOR

1. _____
2. _____
3. _____

## SOMEONE SPECIAL TO ME & WHY

_____

## I FEEL

☐ ☐ ☐ ☐ ☐ ☐

## WHAT WAS GREAT ABOUT TODAY?

_____
_____
_____
_____

DOODLE OF THE DAY!

M  T  W  TH  F  S  SU     DATE: ___ / ___ / ___

## I AM THANKFUL FOR

1. _____
2. _____
3. _____

## SOMEONE SPECIAL TO ME & WHY

_____

I FEEL  ☐  ☐  ☐  ☐  ☐  ☐

## WHAT WAS GREAT ABOUT TODAY?

_____
_____
_____
_____
_____

DOODLE OF THE DAY!

M  T  W  TH  F  S  SU     DATE: ___/___/___

## I AM THANKFUL FOR

1. _____
2. _____
3. _____

## SOMEONE SPECIAL TO ME & WHY

_____

**I FEEL**  ☐  ☐  ☐  ☐  ☐  ☐

## WHAT WAS GREAT ABOUT TODAY?

_____
_____
_____
_____
_____

DOODLE OF THE DAY!

M  T  W  TH  F  S  SU      DATE: __ / __ / __

## I AM THANKFUL FOR

1. _____
2. _____
3. _____

## SOMEONE SPECIAL TO ME & WHY

_____

## I FEEL

☐  ☐  ☐  ☐  ☐  ☐

## WHAT WAS GREAT ABOUT TODAY?

_____
_____
_____
_____
_____

DOODLE OF THE DAY!

M  T  W  TH  F  S  SU     DATE: __ / __ / __

## I AM THANKFUL FOR

1. _____
2. _____
3. _____

## SOMEONE SPECIAL TO ME & WHY

_____

I FEEL  □  □  □  □  □  □

## WHAT WAS GREAT ABOUT TODAY?

_____
_____
_____
_____
_____

DOODLE OF THE DAY!

M  T  W  TH  F  S  SU      DATE: ___ / ___ / ___

## I AM THANKFUL FOR

1. _____
2. _____
3. _____

## SOMEONE SPECIAL TO ME & WHY

_____

## I FEEL
☐  ☐  ☐  ☐  ☐  ☐

## WHAT WAS GREAT ABOUT TODAY?

_____
_____
_____
_____
_____

DOODLE OF THE DAY!

M   T   W   TH   F   S   SU      DATE: ___ / ___ / ___

## I AM THANKFUL FOR

1. _____
2. _____
3. _____

## SOMEONE SPECIAL TO ME & WHY

_____

I FEEL   ☐   ☐   ☐   ☐   ☐   ☐

## WHAT WAS GREAT ABOUT TODAY?

_____
_____
_____
_____
_____

DOODLE OF THE DAY!

# ONE FOR THE GIRLS!
## AVAILABLE ON AMAZON NOW

The life-changing gratitude journal that develops a positive mindset and emotions

Made in the USA
Monee, IL
12 November 2019